Baby Orangutans at the Zoo

Cecelia H. Brannon

Enslow Publishing
101 W. 23rd Street
Suite 240
New York, NY 10011
USA
enslow.com

Published in 2017 by Enslow Publishing, LLC.
101 W. 23rd Street, Suite 240, New York, NY 10011

Library of Congress Cataloging-in-Publication Data

Names: Brannon, Cecelia H., author.
Title: Baby orangutans at the zoo / Cecelia H. Brannon.
Description: New York, NY : Enslow Publishing, 2017. | Series: All about baby zoo animals | Audience: Ages 3+ | Audience: Preschool. | Includes bibliographical references and index.
Identifiers: LCCN 2015044445| ISBN 9780766075696 (library bound) | ISBN 9780766079175 (pbk.) | ISBN 9780766075276 (6-pack)
Subjects: LCSH: Orangutans—Infancy—Juvenile literature. | Zoo animals—Infancy—Juvenile literature.
Classification: LCC QL737.P94 B75 2016 | DDC 599.88/3139—dc23
LC record available at http://lccn.loc.gov/2015044445

Printed in Malaysia

To Our Readers: We have done our best to make sure all websites in this book were active and appropriate when we went to press. However, the author and the publisher have no control over and assume no liability for the material available on those websites or on any websites they may link to. Any comments or suggestions can be sent by e-mail to customerservice@enslow.com.

Photo Credits: Cover, pp. 3 (right), 12 Sergey Lavrentev/Shutterstock.com; p. 1 iStockphoto.com/Craig Dingle; pp. 4–5 iStock.com/BreathFitness; pp. 6, 22 ROLAND WEIHRAUCH/DPA/Getty Images; pp. 3 (center), 8 Kate Capture/Shutterstock.com; p. 10 Joseph Scott Photography/Shutterstock.com; p. 14 iStock.com/Enjoylife2; p. 16 iStock.com/haydenbird; pp. 3 (left), 18 PEDRO ARMSTRE/AFP/ Getty Images; p. 20 Boule/Shutterstock.com.

Contents

Words to Know

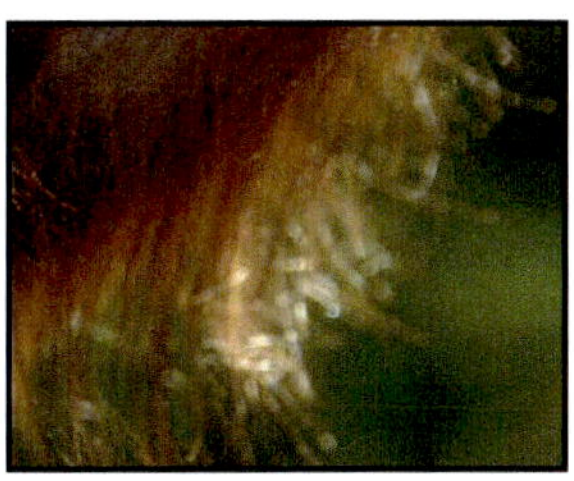
fur

infant

swing

Zo

Who lives at the zoo?

A baby orangutan lives at the zoo!

A baby orangutan is called an infant, just like a human baby!

An orangutan infant is covered with orange fur. When it is born, its skin is pink. As it gets older, its skin turns gray.

An orangutan infant likes to swing and climb. It can hold on with its feet!

An orangutan infant rides on its mother until it can walk on its own.

An orangutan infant drinks milk. It also eats fruits and vegetables, such as yams, bananas, and apples.

An orangutan infant likes to play with toys. It is very smart.

Orangutan infants grunt and howl to talk to other orangutans. They also make a sound called a "kiss-squeak" to show they are excited.

You can see an orangutan infant at the zoo!

Read More

Arnold, Caroline. *Orangutans*. Great Neck, NY: Starwalk Kids Media, 2013.

Mattern, Joanne. *Orangutans (Asian Animals)*. North Mankato, MN: Capstone Press, 2010.

Websites

Discovery Kids: Orangutan
kids.nationalgeographic.com/animals/orangutan/#orangutan-swinging-rope.jpg

San Diego Zoo: Orangutan
kids.sandiegozoo.org/animals/mammals/orangutan

Index

Guided Reading Level: B
Guided Reading Leveling System is based on the guidelines recommended by Fountas and Pinnell.

Word Count: 139